MW00809364

GOD'S PLAN FOR YOU

I want everyone to get ready for "God's Plan for You," written by Tim Outlaw. God has plans for you and your life. Pick up this book today!

—Chuck Norris
ChuckNorris.com

***

I am so grateful that almost twenty years into our friendship, Tim Outlaw is still speaking into my life. I cannot think of a better person to guide each of us towards God's direction. I have watched (at times with horror) as Tim has learned and lived out each of the lessons that he teaches us in this book. This devotional uses Star Wars, Socks and Sandals, and pant-less hunting trips to explain deep concepts about God. If that doesn't pique your interest, I am not sure what will.

That's who Tim has always been. Someone who uses his embarrassing moments and mistakes to make the people around him better…

It is my hope that over the next 21 days, that you too, will lean in and experience the author of your story. I pray that you too, will hear God's voice whispering and prompting your steps. Most of all, I hope that you will experience God's plan for you.

—Zachary Taylor
Pastor. Leader. Speaker.
ZacharyWtaylor.com

"An unexamined life is not worth living" (Socrates) certainly is true of all of us who want to understand God better and grow closer to Him. "God's Plan for You" leads the reader on a fascinating journey of introspection and fresh discovery that is both practical and inspirational as we reassess, refocus, and look to our future with faith. "God's Plan for You" is biblically based, interesting, and worth reading at the start of your day.

—Rev. David Arrol Macfarlane
Author, Ignite Your Life.
DavidaMacfarlane.com

***

The decision to follow Jesus is the greatest decision a person will ever make! When I made a commitment to follow Jesus and give Him my life, I began to consume His Word and any book that could help guide me on my walk with Christ. Accepting Jesus only takes a moment, but becoming His disciple takes a lifetime. Tim Outlaw has written a great guide for any new believer placing their trust in the Lord and desiring to please Him. In this devotional book, a person will get a step-by-step on how to start and continue in their journey with the Lord. I highly recommend this book to be placed in the hands of every new believer!

—Pastor Abram Gomez
AbramGomez.com

***

Tim writes from the heart! A must-read devotional book that everyone should read and study. It is very practical and an easy read for the entire world. His real-life experiences want you to read more and more each day. I highly recommend that you take the time to absorb and meditate on each prayed over thought. Each study is from Tim's heart, and I wanted more and more as I read his book!

—Chuck Watson
MyFathersWork.org

GOD'S PLAN FOR YOU
21-DAY DEVOTIONAL

TIM OUTLAW

Published by KHARIS PUBLISHING, imprint of KHARIS MEDIA LLC.

Copyright © 2020 Timothy W. Outlaw

ISBN-13: 978-1-63746-108-2

ISBN-10: 1-63746-108-9

Library of Congress Control Number: 2022930813

Scripture quotations marked (NIV) are taken from the Holy Bible, New International Version®, NIV®. Copyright © 1973, 1978, 1984, 2011 by Biblica, Inc.™ Used by permission of Zondervan. All rights reserved worldwide. www.zondervan.comThe "NIV" and "New International Version" are trademarks registered in the United States Patent and Trademark Office by Biblica, Inc.™

Scripture quotations are from the ESV® Bible (The Holy Bible, English Standard Version®), copyright © 2001 by Crossway, a publishing ministry of Good News Publishers. Used by permission. All rights reserved.

Scripture quotations taken from the (NASB®) New American Standard Bible®, Copyright © 1960, 1971, 1977, 1995, 2020 by The Lockman Foundation. Used by permission. All rights reserved. www.lockman.org

Scripture quotations marked (NLT) are taken from the Holy Bible, New Living Translation, copyright ©1996, 2004, 2015 by Tyndale House Foundation. Used by permission of Tyndale House Publishers, Carol Stream, Illinois 60188. All rights reserved.

Design by Joshua Jenney, Anna King

Edited by Joann Hawkins, Karen Herceg

All KHARIS PUBLISHING products are available at special quantity discounts for bulk purchase for sales promotions, premiums, fund-raising, and educational needs. For details, contact:

Kharis Media LLC
Tel: 1-479-599-8657
support@kharispublishing.com
www.kharispublishing.com

Special thanks to my wife Sara
for all her prayers, assistance, and
continual encouragement.

TABLE OF CONTENTS

FOREWORD

As a pastor, the most common question I am always asked is, "What is God's plan for my life?" Unfortunately for the people that I pastor, I always tell them that they're probably asking the wrong person.

There is something inside each of us that intuitively feels a destiny written into our hearts. And yet, every single one of us has felt a disconnect, or maybe even a disappointment, in the discovery process of that purpose. Has anyone else ever felt stuck in life? Unsure of what's next? Has anyone else been frozen in indecision? If so, this book is for you.

Some of my most agonizing moments have been sitting and waiting while trying to hear what direction God had for my life. Even as I spent time over the last 21 days reading this devotional, I realized that I was once again struggling with one of those agonizing decisions!!! It wasn't until I got to Day Twelve or Thirteen that the consistent lesson began to ring true. God's plan for my life is more about leaning into the author of my story than it is about the next decision I am making *in* that story.

I am so grateful that almost twenty years into our friendship Tim Outlaw is still speaking into my life. I cannot think of a better person to guide each of us towards God's direction. I have watched (at times with horror) as Tim has learned and lived out each of the lessons that he teaches us in this book. This devotional uses Star Wars, Socks and Sandals, and pant-less hunting trips to explain deep concepts about God. If that doesn't pique your interest, I am not sure what will.

That's who Tim has always been. Someone who uses his embarrassing moments and mistakes to make the people around him better. One of my favorite moments was the day he convinced me to allow him to take my brand-new motorcycle out for a ride. Fifteen seconds later, my bike zigged, zagged and was completely wrecked. There is a YouTube video out there somewhere to prove it! (By the way, Tim still owes me back for the damages.) If you will allow it, I have no doubt that this devotional will take you for a ride. It will zig and it will zag as it uses some of the simplest things in life to show you that God has something special for you. Even more importantly, it will show you that God *sees* something special in you.

It is my hope that over the next 21 days you, too, will lean in and experience the author of your story. I pray that you, too, will hear God's voice whispering and prompting your steps. Most of all, I hope that you will experience God's plan for you.

Zachary Taylor
Pastor. Leader. Speaker.
ZacharyWtaylor.com

INTRODUCTION

Raised in Miami, Florida as a pastor's kid, I grew up in the church; I knew the reality of God. But I fell away from the church from 18 to 20 years old. When I became involved in church again one of my main incentives was to meet women. With all the wrong motives, I read my Bible, got incredibly involved in the church, and got serious about prayer. I felt I had to be seen as a guy who did all these things in order to get the kind of woman I wanted. After all, it's hard to be seen as a good, righteous person if you show up to Bible study without having done the assigned reading, right?

There was this slow progression in my life that I didn't really notice at first. Then, about 18 months into all this, something changed. The desires of my heart changed. My heart and my life were transformed. No longer was I going to church or reading my Bible to impress women; instead, to know God and serve Him became the desires of my heart! My heart now longs to serve God, and to see people changed by Him. God put a new heart and a new spirit into me, and He can do it for you, too!

In 2006 I took my first full-time position in ministry. That same year I was encouraged repeatedly by the words, "God has plans for you." Little did I know that over the next 15 years God would send me on a journey ministering in 32 states and eight nations! I gained experience applying God's word to difficult situations in various cultures. During the Covid-19 Pandemic of 2020, I felt God's plan for me was to write this book, and to share the experience and wisdom I have gained in how to pursue God's personal plan for every Christ follower.

God wants your passions, goals, and direction in life to align with His.

God has a plan for your life. His plan will not likely make you a multi-millionaire or give you everything you want (just as good parents are careful not to spoil their children). No, God's plan for you is much more significant. As God gives you a new heart, it becomes obvious the world needs what God gave you—love, grace, and redemption. The world must know this new heart and spirit you have! God's plan might include you telling hundreds of people what He has done for you; or God's plan might include you running the sound board at church. But one thing God's plan includes is this: loving people you think you do not like.

My hope is that by the end of these 21 days you will have the confidence to know God's will for your life and as Romans says: to test and approve what God's will is.

Watch the videos of "God's Plan for Me" for free at youtube.com/n2nstudios

DAY 1

FEELINGS OR TRUTH

The heart is more deceitful than all else
And is desperately sick;
Who can understand it?
-Jeremiah 17:9, NASB

In *Star Wars the Empire Strikes Back*, there is one of the most iconic scenes in cinema history. In case you don't know it, in this movie the bad guy, Darth Vader, tells the good guy, Luke Skywalker, "I am your father." Luke says, "No, that's impossible." To which Darth Vader says, "Search your feelings; you know it to be true." Then Luke screeches, "NOOO!"

Unfortunately, this is how much of the world and even Christians believe truth works. Many think, "I feel it's true, so it must be true." That is a lie! As we read in Jeremiah, the heart (which many of us think of as the source of our emotions) is deceitful above all else and desperately sick.

My first professional job was selling satellite TV. I made good money. I was good at it and even received top sales marks. If I listened to everything I felt was true or

1

accepted what everyone told me as truth, I would likely still be selling satellite TV and living a mediocre life today. However, I didn't listen to my ego which said, "Get rich!" Instead, I listened first and foremost to the Bible, to the truth God has revealed to us—to be God's witnesses to the ends of the earth and to go forth and make disciples. I have already done far more than I thought possible in my life because I focused on the truth revealed in the Word of God. We always, always, always, start with revealed truth in the Holy Bible! Let's look at some more truth. The end of Romans 12:2 says, "Then you will be able to test and approve what God's will is—His good, pleasing and perfect will."

Take a few minutes right now and think about any life decisions you may be struggling with. Once you have identified a few, write them down. We will reference these several times throughout the next 21 days, so take some time to consider real decisions you're facing.

Think About It:

Life decisions I am struggling with right now:

Dating, career, moving, church/community involvement, broken relationship etc.

_____

_____

_____

_____

_____

_____

_____

Now that you have identified areas where you need God's guidance, lift those things up in prayer.

Pray:

Heavenly Father, I acknowledge I need You. I can often be led by my feelings, and I want to be led by truth. Convict me when I'm heading in the wrong direction and help me to open up my heart and fill it with truth.

Walk It Out:

This week take note of the decisions you make. Ask yourself, "Did I decide this based on how I felt or based on what God's Word says?"

DAY 2

GET IN THE GAME

Therefore, I urge you, brothers and sisters, in view of God's mercy, to offer your bodies as a living sacrifice, holy and pleasing to God—this is your true and proper worship.
-Romans 12:1, NIV

Today we're going to focus on the first part of the verse: God's mercy. What is mercy? Mercy is withholding punishment from someone when punishment is due.

If you're reading this book, there's a strong chance you've received God's mercy and have a relationship with God. That's great news because this is the most vital step in discovering God's plan for your life. We can't move toward our purpose unless we have God's mercy in our lives.

We as Christ followers need to walk in step with God's mercy. They go together like peanut butter and jelly, bees and honey, shoes and socks. You get the picture. Once you receive God's mercy and have a relationship with Jesus, you can begin to pursue God's plan for your life.

I've heard it explained like this: There's a game God wants you to play (not a literal game; it's an illustration of God's plan for you). Let's say football for instance. There are 22 guys on the field, and you are one of thousands watching from the stands. If you walk up to the coach and say, "Hey what's the game plan?" he's going to say, "Who are you?" He doesn't have that relationship with you; he's not going to give you the plan for the game. He's most definitely *not* putting you in the game with an important role. But we know from 1 Timothy Chapter 2 that God desires all people to be saved and come to the knowledge of truth. In this illustration that would be like the coach calling into the stands, telling you to get into this game!

Accepting God's mercy gets us in the game.

The first step you need in order to know the game plan and get to know God's will for your life is to repent, turn from your sin, turn to God, and submit your life to Jesus Christ. You must receive His mercy. This is how you get into the game!

Think About It:

- Who do I need to show mercy to?

- How can I better reflect God's mercy?

- When did I first turn from my sin and turn to God and receive His mercy?

   Think about this and write a brief summary:

E.g., Youth group, a revival, my friend shared Jesus with me, etc.

_____

_____

_____

_____

_____

_____

_____

_____

_____

Pray:

Lord God, I thank You for Your mercy. Help me to reflect the mercies You have given me.

Walk It Out:

Next time someone wrongs you, remember Christ's mercy for you. Show them mercy.

DAY 3

SUBMIT

Therefore, I urge you, brothers and sisters, in view of God's mercy, to offer your bodies as a living sacrifice, holy and pleasing to God—this is your true and proper worship.
-Romans 12:1, NIV

Following "…in view of God's mercy," this passage says, "to offer your bodies as a living sacrifice, holy and pleasing to God." Simply put, this means offer yourself fully to Jesus—submit to Jesus. As we remember Christ's mercy and His blood shed on the cross, we submit our wills to His. For some crazy reason we often tend to think our ideas and plans are "better" than His. Maybe they are easier or maybe we are just more comfortable with them. If you want to know God's plans for you, you must submit to Jesus. Simply ask yourself, "Have I offered this to Jesus?" Have I offered this relationship, this hobby, this career, this ministry opportunity—to Jesus?

I was 17 at a Church camp when I told God my life was His and I would do whatever He wanted me to do. I did not know fully what that meant at 17, and I was not obedient to it. Fast forward a few years. I had a good-paying sales job. For a guy my age with no college education at the time, it was very good pay. In that season of my life, I was beginning to grow much closer to God. I remembered my prayer at 17 and understood more fully what it meant. A job in ministry came up. It paid a quarter of what I was currently making. This was the kind of financial decision that puts you in a panic! What should I do? Through a process of prayer, Bible study, and talking to mentors, the answer became obvious. Taking the one peanut-a-day job was good because it was God's plan for me. And it ended up being my first step into ministry as I began sharing the Gospel in assemblies around the U.S.

Looking back, that step to begin working in ministry was one of the greatest and most fulfilling decisions of my life. It was obvious what God wanted me to do because I was submitted to Him. Offer your plans to God, and He will make it clear. It probably won't be easy, but it will be clear.

If receiving God's Mercy gets you in the game, submission to Jesus tells you the game you're playing (like knowing whether you're playing soccer, basketball, baseball, etc.) It reveals what you're made for. You are submitted to Jesus Christ, and you're playing for Him. His teachings, rules and precepts are what govern this game plan for your life.

Think About It:

- Have I ever felt that my personal plans were better than what God might have for me? Why?

- What plans have I submitted to Jesus?

- Am I fully submitted to Jesus? Have I offered my body as a living sacrifice as Romans says?

Pray:

Father, I acknowledge Your plans are better than my own. Help me to submit to You and Your will more fully.

Walk It Out:

Reference the life decisions you wrote down on day 1. Surrender those life decisions to Jesus right now and continue doing this in prayer every day until He gives you an answer to those plans.

Notes:

_____

_____

_____

_____

_____

DAY 4

WORLDLY OR GODLY?

Do not conform to the pattern of this world, but be transformed by the renewing of your mind. Then you will be able to test and approve what God's will is—his good, pleasing and perfect will.
-Romans 12:2, NIV

What does it mean to conform to the world, and how do we, as Christians, do the opposite? Not conforming to the world means, not being molded by fleeting fashion, not focusing on pursuing pleasure, not conforming to the idea that comfortable living (making a lot of money, living for yourself, etc.) is the goal in life. Not that pleasure or nice living is a sin, but if that is our focus in life, we would have the same focus as many atheists who think they should live it up now because there is no afterlife. Do not be molded by these things.

Let's start at the top of the verse: "Do not conform to the pattern of this world." This is almost a subpoint to submitting to Jesus. The Apostle Paul specifically tells us here *not* to conform to the world. Some of you may hear this and think of it as, "Don't sin." Conforming to the

10

world covers sin, but it also covers a lot more. The obvious focus here would be sin: do not get drunk, gossip, lie, use God's name in vain, etc. The interesting thing is that Paul does not actually say, "Don't sin, everybody." Here he says not to conform to the pattern of the world.

To help us know what is worldly, I encourage you to put every plan into two categories: worldly or godly. To figure out which it is, ask yourself this simple question: "Is this biblical?" Let's do one together. Let us examine dating/courting a non-Christian; it must fall into one of these categories: worldly or godly. So, we ask ourselves, "Is dating a non-Christian biblical?" Or, in other words, can we use the patterns of Scripture (not just one isolated verse) to see that this is God's heart for His children? 2 Corinthians tells us not to be unequally yoked, which means not to be tied together in marriage with unbelievers. If you are in Christ, you have no business being in a romantic relationship with a non-Christian. This absolutely belongs in the worldly category.

I was once put in a job with a very gray area. I assisted with paperwork and was expected to follow the shady standard everyone else in the industry followed. Paperwork would be turned in to me. The paperwork was to make sure we followed government regulations; however, the paperwork usually reflected that we did not follow the regulations. My job was to change the paperwork to make everything look legal instead of illegal, so that the company and staff didn't get fined for breaking the law. Falsifying the documents was perceived by everyone in the company as normal and necessary. As Romans 2 tells us, our conscience bears witness, and even though everyone said this was okay, I saw it as lying. I could have been molded by the world and said this is normal. But when I asked myself, "Is what I'm doing biblical?" the answer was a clear no. The Ten

Commandments tell us not to lie; I saw it as lying, and my conscience bore witness (Romans 2:15) to that. So, I quit that job.

Think About It:

- What worldly things influence me the most? Movies, music, my phone, people, etc.

- How can I begin to change that?

- Why is it hard to go against the pattern of the world?

Pray:

Lord, I know there are patterns of this world that shape me. Help me to be molded by You instead of the world.

Walk It Out:

Reference the life decisions you wrote down on Day 1. Ask yourself, "Is it worldly or godly?" Remember that we determine this by simply asking, "Is this biblical?" This helps direct us to God's best for us. If you have trouble with this step, call a leader in your church to walk you through this.

Notes:

_____

_____

_____

_____

DAY 5

BE TRANSFORMED

Do not conform to the pattern of this world, but be transformed by the renewing of your mind. Then you will be able to test and approve what God's will is—his good, pleasing and perfect will.
-Romans 12:2, NIV

In *Star Wars*, Jedi Master Yoda says, "You must unlearn what you have learned." This quote relays what we need to take from this Bible passage. Unlearn all the junk from the world; be transformed by God's Word and the Holy Spirit. As Christians we are not to be molded by the world but by the Word of God! We are transformed by reading and applying God's Word, first and foremost.

Remember Day 1 when Jeremiah 17:9 tells us the heart is deceitful. That's why being transformed by the renewing of your mind is so important. You must forget everything the world teaches and cling to what God's word says. God is not just going to change your heart— He is going to make it new. It is a process.

For example, you don't go on a diet for a week and become magically fit. When I was 14, I weighed 240lbs with probably not a pound of muscle. I wanted to play football. That meant some drastic changes in my life. It started with cutting out soda. Then backing off on sweets. I began lifting weights and running. I rather quickly dropped to 190lbs, and by 16 I was playing football. I was not remotely the fastest, strongest, or most skilled. So, I took it up another notch. I would eat wheat grass for breakfast, run to the gym (literally, I ran 1.4 miles to the gym), lift weights for 90 minutes, and run another mile and a half back home. I would take a nap, which is important for muscles to rebuild, then go about my day ending with a serious run of six miles. By the time I was 19, I weighed 210lbs (all that weight being muscle), and I could bench press 300lbs and easily run a mile in under 6 minutes. It took five years and drastic changes to how I lived my life, but an obvious transformation took place. Likewise, being transformed by God's Word doesn't happen in 5 minutes a day. I pray you apply the walk-it-out section today and let God begin to transform your life!

Think About It:

- Can I be transformed by God's Word if I'm not open to change? Why?

- How has God transformed me already?

- As Romans says, be transformed by the renewing of your mind. What habits can I start in order to begin that process?

Pray:

Father, thank You for offering to change me and to make my heart and mind new. Thank You for Your powerful Word and Holy Spirit doing this good work in me as I cooperate with you.

Walk It Out:

If you are not spending daily time with God outside this book, prepare to spend daily time with God so you can fast-track renewing of your mind.

Where: my bedroom, etc.

When: 6:45 a.m., etc.

How: spend five minutes in prayer, follow a Bible-in-a-year reading plan, etc.

DAY 6

TEST AND APPROVE

Therefore, I urge you, brothers and sisters, in view of God's mercy, to offer your bodies as a living sacrifice, holy and pleasing to God—this is your true and proper worship. Do not conform to the pattern of this world, but be transformed by the renewing of your mind. Then you will be able to test and approve what God's will is—his good, pleasing and perfect will.
-Romans 12:1-2, NIV

This is our final day in Romans. This is an extraordinarily rich passage that required several days to chew on mentally. One thing we have yet to address is the first word of the passage: "Therefore." This word is important as it ties together the previous 11 chapters of Romans that thoroughly establish the Gospel of Jesus Christ! Everything we read in today's passage is because God had mercy on us and sent Christ to pay the penalty for our sins with His blood shed on the cross. Would you remember that and read the above passage again?

We have forgiveness of our sins; we have eternal life and relationship with God! God gives us all of that, and this passage says, in light of that, we are called to be a living sacrifice because this is true and proper worship. This requires us to submit our plans, our ideas and, yes, our lives to Jesus. We are commanded, yes commanded, not to conform to the world but to be transformed through Scripture and the Holy Spirit. Then we will be able to test and know God's will.

Now that we have gone over how to test and approve God's will, why are the next 15 days necessary? Transformation by renewal of your mind is a lifelong process.

Several years ago, I bought a prefab kitchen island, which basically means it came in a box and I had to put it together. It had a butcher block on top for cutting and a cabinet below for storage. It looked very simple to assemble. It came in several pieces. I took a quick glance at the instructions and attempted to put it together. Quickly, I realized this wasn't simple. There were 38 packs of various nuts, bolts, screws, and connectors—not 38 screws total, 38 *packs* of screws and bolts! In the first hour I referenced the instructions over a dozen times. I thought I would be able to take a quick glance at them and it would all be straightforward. It was not. It is the same when it comes to our lives.

By now, you likely have a proper understanding of Romans 12:1-2. Don't fool yourself into thinking you have all the answers to test and approve every decision you may have to make. A quick glance at Scripture will not help you put your life together. Having a relationship with God will. As you meditate on God's Word and talk to His Spirit, this relationship will transform you and renew your mind.

Think About It:

- Reflect on all God has given you, including His mercy, salvation, relationship with Jesus, and the ability to know His will for your life.

- What is the hardest part of this passage to live out? Why?

Pray:

Lord God, thank You for my relationship with You. Thank You for all You have given me. May my life be true and proper worship to You.

Walk It Out:

In your own words, write how to test and approve God's will.

_____

_____

_____

_____

_____

_____

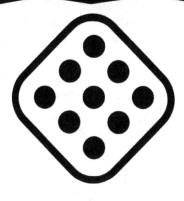

DAY 7

MEASURING STICK

Finally, brothers and sisters, whatever is true, whatever is noble, whatever is right, whatever is pure, whatever is lovely, whatever is admirable—if anything is excellent or praiseworthy—think about such things.
-Philippians 4:8, NIV

"Measure twice, cut once." If you have ever cut a piece of wood, you've heard this saying. I was once making cabinet drawers with my brother. He must have said that phrase half a dozen times. Still, somehow, we had some bad cuts. It was amazing to me how less than 1/16th of an inch could keep a drawer from fitting properly. Likewise, God's Word is full of passages we can use as "measuring sticks" to see if something "fits" in our lives. One of my favorites is Philippians 4:8. This passage tells us to think about things that are noble, right, pure, lovely, admirable, excellent, and praiseworthy.

Let's walk this out. Let's say you have two choices on a Sunday evening. The first is to go to church youth group, and the other is to spend time with a friend going through a rough time and who isn't following God. If we meditate on Philippians 4:8 and pray about this situation, one choice will likely become very clear. What is God's best for you? I am sure many of you thought right away, "Obviously, the thing that is right, pure, and lovely is to go to church with other Christians". However, I know some people reading this thought, "The most excellent and praiseworthy response is to bring Christ to those who don't know Him."

Recently, my wife and I experienced this scenario. As we prayed about it and thought of this verse, my wife decided to go and be with her friend while I went to church.

God's best for you may not be identical to what it would be for your friend.

God has options for you, but His Word and His Spirit will direct us to His best. So, meditate on passages like Philippians 4:8 to determine if your choice measures up to God's best for your life.

Think About It:

- Think of some things that are noble, right, pure, lovely, admirable, excellent, and praiseworthy.

Pray:

Father God, help me in my choices to choose wisely things that measure up to what You desire for me.

Walk It Out:

Look back at Day 1 and the choices you are struggling with. Contrast it with Philippians 4:8 to see where these decisions measure up.

Notes:

_____

_____

_____

_____

_____

_____

_____

_____

_____

DAY 8

DESIRES OF YOUR HEART

Delight yourself in the Lord; And he will give you the desires of your heart.
-Psalm 37:4, NASB

I have a two-year-old son, and he loves cookies! He will do almost anything for a cookie. He will eat his vegetables and clean up his toys; he will even go to bed without a fuss for the promise of a cookie the next day. I think we can all relate to wanting something so badly we'll do just about anything for it.

In today's verse, we probably all tend to focus on the end, "He will give you the desires of your heart," much like my two-year-old wanting a cookie. However, the beginning of the verse is important, too: "Delight yourself in the Lord." What does it mean to delight ourselves in God?

The people we enjoy spending time with influence us the most. We can become like them, unconsciously mimicking or copying them in many ways. If we "delight" in the Lord and spend a lot of time with Him, He changes us and we become like Him!

My wife likes to eat healthy, watch romantic comedies, and listen to Christian Metal. When we met, these were things I almost never did. After years of marriage, I now eat salads five times a week, I can enjoy a romantic comedy with my wife on occasion, and I even tolerate the metal music. Delight in the Lord, and He will give you the desires of your heart.

Let's say you want a $100,000 sports car and begin to delight in the Lord. In my experience it is unlikely God is going to give you a $100,000 sports car. If you are truly delighting in the Lord, He is making changes on your heart–and the desires of your heart change. Instead of desiring a $100,000 sports car, you may start having the desire to give money to the poor.

You do not live out this verse for the cookie; you do it because it is a delight to live it out. It's a joy to know God and to feel God's love for you–changing you.

Think About It:

- Do I delight in the Lord?

- How has the time I spend in prayer and in the Bible influenced my heart's desires?

Pray:

Lord, help me not to be selfish but to be selfless, and help me reflect You more closely as I seek to delight in Your presence.

Walk It Out:

Make a plan; How can I delight in the Lord? How can I make spending time with God through prayer and Bible study more enjoyable?

Join or start a Bible Study, listen to preaching/teaching on my drive to work, listen to worship music while jogging,

memorize scripture with friends, decorate part of my home

specifically, to be the place where I spend time with God each day, etc.

_____

_____

_____

_____

_____

_____

_____

DAY 9

READ THE ROOM

But Jesus, knowing what they were thinking in their hearts . . .
-Luke 9:47a, NASB

As a former leader of a college group, on ministry nights I always tried to get a "read" on the room—is anyone being left out? Who is talking to whom? Is anyone looking sad, lonely? One evening, this young man named Winston caught my attention. He was usually very social, but that night I noticed him sitting at a table by himself. Everyone was sitting at other tables eating pizza. There were plenty of people there, and they normally made everyone feel welcome and included. But he was alone.

So, I went to sit beside him and, immediately, I knew what was wrong. Not because the Holy Spirit gave me great discernment, and not because the Lord spoke anything special in that moment. I knew because Winston had horrid body odor. In Winston's defense, he had begun riding his bicycle to church, and this was in an area of Texas where it is extremely hot. So, I asked Winston, "How close are we?" He gave me a puzzled look. I said, "Could I tell you if you smelled?" Reluctantly, he said, "I guess so." I said emphatically, "You smell. I keep spray deodorant in my office, top desk drawer." Later, Winston and I became very close. I sometimes wonder what might have happened if I had not been trying to get a read on the room. What would have happened if I had not sat next to Winston and given him deodorant? I mainly wonder all this because Winston would later introduce me to Sara, who is now my wife!

There is a voice from God. I believe God's voice has a read on the room and, more importantly, on us and our hearts. We see His voice expressed in many ways throughout Scripture. Countless times in Scripture we see, "The Word of the Lord came to…." (Esther, Isaiah, Jeremiah, and many others.) We see God speak through Balaam's donkey. We see God speak to Job in a whirlwind, and yet He speaks to Elijah in a still, small voice. God reads the room. He knows the atmosphere of the situations in our lives, what we need to hear, and what will speak most powerfully to our situation. In Luke 9 it says, "But Jesus, knowing what they were thinking in their hearts…."

Jesus knows the reasoning of your heart. Maybe He has not told you "No" because you are not ready to receive it. Maybe He has not told you "Yes" because the timing is not right for you. Maybe He has not spoken to you because you have yet to be quiet and listen.

Think About It:

- Knowing where I am in life and what I am going through, how would I want someone to talk with me? For example: gently, just listening, with positive words, etc.

- How do I expect God in His infinite wisdom to speak to me?

- Do I take enough time to be quiet and listen for God to speak to me?

Pray:

Heavenly Father, please speak to me. Help me to be quiet and listen to Your voice and receive what You are telling me.

Walk It Out:

Read Luke 9:44-50 and remember when you read the Bible that it is God speaking to you. Treat your reading like having a conversation with a friend.

Notes:

_____

_____

_____

_____

_____

_____

_____

DAY 10

ASK QUESTIONS

And the angel of the Lord appeared to him and said to him, "The Lord is with you, O mighty man of valor." And Gideon said to him, "Please, my lord, if the Lord is with us, why then has all this happened to us? And where are all his wonderful deeds that our fathers recounted to us, saying, 'Did not the Lord bring us up from Egypt?' But now the Lord has forsaken us and given us into the hand of Midian."
Judges 6:12-13, ESV

Read Judges 6:11-17

Gideon asked questions. Questions are okay. Questions are good. Ask questions. Gideon asked some very bold ones.

A year into dating Sara (that girl Winston introduced me to), I was thinking about marrying her. One very cold day, I decided to go for walk to a nearby pond and talk with God about her. By the time I got to the pond, I wanted to go back because it was so cold, but I knelt there and began to pray. The only agenda or outcome I was hoping for was just to remain in the center of God's will

28

for my life. Obviously, since marriage is a lifelong commitment, it is serious business and needs proper prayer and consideration. I definitely wanted to marry Sara, but I didn't want to move forward, unless I was positive this was part of God's plan for my life. I was there at the pond kneeling and praying and freezing. I do not remember exactly what I prayed, but I said something like, "God, I don't want to marry her unless it's Your will." Two things happened simultaneously. Like Elijah, I heard a still small voice. It said, "Tim, you know the answer." While I heard this voice, warmth covered me, comforting me. I remember touching my back and arms, at first in surprise, trying to understand how that was happening. Quickly, I realized God was speaking supernaturally to me. I left that park with a huge smile on my face, knowing confidently that God had a plan for me and Sara in marriage.

Ask questions. God has answers for you!

Think About It:

- When I ask God questions, do I expect answers?

- Do I ask God about things that are on my mind?

- Do I ask God specific questions or vague questions?

Pray:

Father, thank You for hearing me.

Walk It Out:

Right now, ask God about all the things on your mind. Ask Him questions as specifically as possible and expect Him to respond.

Notes:

_____

_____

_____

_____

_____

_____

_____

_____

_____

_____

_____

_____

DAY 11

PURPLE SWEATER

But he answered them, "An evil and adulterous generation seeks for a sign, but no sign will be given to it except the sign of the prophet Jonah."
-Matthew 12:39, ESV

This story starts with me at 17 years old attending a high school in Florida. I felt I had a serious relationship with Jesus, but I was young and still developing emotionally and mentally. As with any young man at this age, girls were heavy on my mind. The problem was: there were two girls. Now, I was not dating both girls, but I was definitely interested in both and they were interested in me. So, being a "mature" 17-year-old Christian, I prayed about this. Being very naive and young, this is how I prayed: "Dear Lord, please show me what girl you have for me by having her wear purple tomorrow."

I told you I was very naive for my age. To me this could only go one of two ways: Girl A wears purple or Girl B wears purple—or neither one wears purple. God answered this prayer extremely loudly and checked off an option I did not see coming.

First, I need to explain why I chose purple. My school had a dress code, and purple was not normally allowed. The uniform was khaki, green, and blue. This was in Florida, which is very hot, and this happened in the typically hot month of September. When I woke up, it was cold outside. I had to put on a jacket. I didn't think much of it. Girl A and Girl B were in my second class of the day. I very quickly headed to that class in anticipation. I was the first student to arrive that day. I thought to myself, "Today is the day the Lord will reveal my bride to me!" Girl A came into class first, and I was ecstatic to see that she had a long sleeve purple shirt on! Hallelujah! While I was still taking that in and celebrating, Girl B entered the class with a purple fleece on! I was very disturbed at first. "God, isn't polygamy wrong?" Then another girl, who I had not been praying about, walked in wearing a purple jacket. Then another girl came in with purple socks. Another girl walked in with purple-striped winter wear. My logic went like this: "Ok, which one is wearing the most purple?" As the day went on and I went to more classes, I saw even more girls wearing purple. As it turned out, we were allowed to wear whatever jackets, sweaters, or winter gear we had because of the weather. So many girls were wearing purple. It was unbelievable. I left school that day very confused.

It took me years to figure out what God was saying through that "miracle." Again, I was not that savvy back then. The first thing that is extremely clear to me now is that I had not yet met my bride. Second, I realized that I should not limit God to "A or B, yes or no." His ways aren't our ways. Ask God open-ended questions about your life. Ask these questions and build your relationship with God. A prayer in faith does not need to ask for a sign.

God does not need your request or your permission to give you a sign. God does desire that we know Him, and every good relationship asks questions. Ask questions and expect God to respond.

Think About It:

- Do I desire "a sign" for things I already feel God prompting me to do? Why?

- Do I ask God open-ended questions? Why?

- Why does Jesus say not to seek a sign, but God still provides signs to so many?

Pray:

Lord God, forgive me if I sometimes ask You whether or not to choose "A or B," when You want to tell me something different entirely. I thank You that You are near and personal and not far off.

Walk It Out:

Reference Week 1 and ask God, in as much detail as possible, what He would like you to do regarding the things on the list.

Notes:

_____

_____

_____

_____

_____

DAY 12

EXPECT RESPONSES

When Gideon realized that it was the angel of the Lord, he exclaimed, "Alas, Sovereign Lord! I have seen the angel of the Lord face to face!"
-Judges 6:22, NIV

Read Judges 6:18-22

Sometimes life can be complex and confusing. Thankfully, God deeply cares about each of us and responds in a personal way. When my wife and I found out she was pregnant with our first child, I was working full-time with Nation-2-Nation (a ministry that empowers leaders around the world), and I had also just taken an additional position as Youth Pastor at my home church.

Soon after I became the Youth Pastor, we felt the Lord prompting us to move 300 miles away to expand our work with Nation-2-Nation. The timing made no sense to us, especially since we felt I'd been led by God to the Youth Pastor position. Nevertheless, God was stirring something in my spirit. God confirmed what He was telling us again and again. He did things such as providing a free office space for me in Houston!

So, I kept sensing that God wanted us to take a step of faith regarding all of this. We decided to make an exploratory trip 300 miles away with a three-month old baby. Why? Because God said go, and we expected Him to respond. We planned that trip with virtually no agenda, and yet we ended up meeting three pastors and training 100 missionaries in those three days! A good day for us in ministry might be equipping one or two pastors or missionaries—not 100! God showed up in a huge way. This helped confirm the next step we should take. We spent two years bringing all this before God before moving 300 miles away. We followed God's lead step by step, much as we see in the story of Gideon.

Expect God to respond.

In today's Scripture, Gideon expected a response from God. He prepared an offering. He expected God to take his offering–and God did! Fire came and consumed Gideon's offering, confirming it was the Lord.

Expecting a response when we talk to God is a pattern that we see all throughout Scripture. You need to have faith that God will respond to you. If you continue the story, you'll see God leads Gideon step by step. One step at a time. The same is true for us today.

Think About It:

- Do I always expect God to respond to my prayer?

- Do I go out of my way or take risks of faith expecting God to respond?

  E.g., going on a mission trip and needing to raise money, making dinner to reach out to others in need, serving where I'm uncomfortable, etc.

Pray:

Father, thank You that You are attentive and I can be confident You will respond.

Walk It Out:

Put yourself in a situation where if God does not respond, you will fail. This could be going on a mission trip when you do not know how you are going to pay for it, or how you are going to get the time off for it. Or it could be trying to reconcile a relationship with someone who has not wanted to talk to you for some time.

Notes:

_____

_____

_____

_____

_____

_____

_____

DAY 13

BE OBEDIENT

So, Gideon took ten men of his servants and did as
the Lord had told him.
-Judges 6:27a, ESV

Read Judges 6:25-27

When I was 22, I started a full-time job in ministry traveling around the nation. While traveling, I thought a lot about how there was a huge lack of outreach and discipleship for young people like me back in my hometown in Texas. Then I attended a Thursday night worship service in Colorado for 18-25-year-olds. There were thousands of 18-25-years-olds there worshipping Jesus. Apparently, this church held this event every Thursday night. I was in awe.

I began talking to God. "God, why isn't this in my hometown?" I asked. I knew that what I heard back was from God, because I would've never thought of it on my own. I heard an echo of my own voice: "Tim, why isn't this in your hometown?" This made me very emotional. I shed some tears. I sat down while everyone else was standing and worshipping. I became uncomfortable and confused at first. I thought, "Surely, God is not asking me to start a ministry. I'm only 22." This is where I can relate heavily to Gideon. I am the least in my father's house, my clan is the weakest, Gideon cried. "God, there are better men to do what you're asking me to do." I thought about all of this for days, then I called my youth pastor, a guy who had helped push me into ministry. I told him what God had put on my heart. Part of me wanted to hear, "Tim you can't do that." He said, "I think this is from the Lord." I finished the commitment to my current job and the following year I started a college ministry.

Being obedient to what God told me was difficult. However, it shaped me in incredibly positive and continuing ways. I made many lasting relationships, including meeting my wife. People came to faith in Christ, and many more became extremely serious about relationships with Jesus. Through my obedience, I became closer to God. I saw God provide in many ways, which caused me to turn to Him, rely on Him and trust Him more. The time I spent with the Bible became less a "chore" and grew much more into a joy! Through this ever-improving intimacy with God, His will for my life became increasingly clear.

What if I had not been obedient to what God had said?

I have no idea what my life would look like if I had not been obedient to what God said. I do know what it looks like because of my obedience, and even though there have been many difficulties God has asked me to face, I am stronger because of them.

Think About It:

- Am I willing to be obedient if God asks me to do something I don't want to do?

- What person(s) will help me walk out obedience if I'm hesitant?

- What reservation(s) keep me from doing what God asks of me?

Pray:

Father God, help my unbelief and doubt. Convict me and strengthen me to do Your will.

Walk It Out:

When you feel God prompting you to action, share it with someone trustworthy to keep you accountable.

Notes:

_____

_____

_____

_____

_____

_____

DAY 14

CONSEQUENCES

Now the word of the Lord came to Jonah the son of Amittai, saying, "Arise, go to Nineveh, that great city, and call out against it, for their evil has come up before me." But Jonah rose to flee to Tarshish from the presence of the Lord. He went down to Joppa and found a ship going to Tarshish. So he paid the fare and went down into it, to go with them to Tarshish, away from the presence of the Lord.
-Jonah 1:1-3, ESV

And the Lord appointed a great fish to swallow up Jonah. And Jonah was in the belly of the fish three days and three nights.
-Jonah 1:17, ESV

Read Jonah Chapter 1

God told Jonah to go to Nineveh. Jonah went in the opposite direction. As we read the story, it is clear there are consequences when we do not listen to God. Reading the whole book of Jonah, we also see, ultimately, Jonah does what is asked of him. A mentor of my wife likes to say, "The safest place to be is in the center of God's will. You don't need to be in the ocean for God to send a fish to swallow you up."

I don't know what will happen if you are not obedient to what God says, I can only tell you there are consequences. God is good and wants what is best for you. My son has had difficulty learning not to throw things. To teach him how harmful throwing can be, we take away his favorite toy and put it in a "timeout." Our son must learn the consequences of his actions and learn what is best.

God does the same for you and me.

Hebrews 12:6, ESV

For the Lord disciplines the one he loves, and chastises every son whom he receives.

Think About It:

- When have I been disciplined by God?

- Have I ever wanted to run in the opposite direction of where God called me? Why?

Pray:

Father, thank You for loving me enough to discipline me and keep me on the right path.

Walk It Out:

Consider whether you may be in the middle of the consequences of rejecting God's plans for your life. If so, repent! Ask for forgiveness and run in the right direction God has called you to!

Consider being in the middle of God's will as the safest place you can be, even if it is a war zone or a place you despise. Look back over your notes from Day 1, considering these things.

Notes:

_____

_____

_____

_____

_____

_____

_____

_____

_____

_____

_____

DAY 15

OBVIOUS, NOT EASY

Your word is a lamp to my feet
And a light to my path.
-Psalm 119:105, NASB

My first hunting trip taught me a lot about staying on the path. Back in college, my roommate and I had done a lot of planning and scouting of the location for our first day of hunting at a wildlife refuge. We had planned to set up several hundred yards away from each other. The beaten-down path we planned to take was obvious in the daytime but harder to find as the sun set. This wildlife refuge had a lot of thick brush more than 12 feet high and full of thorns. If we walked off the path, we could easily get lost or cornered by the tall, thick, brush.

On the first day of the hunt, we arrived as early as possible, while it was still dark outside. As planned, we separated, each of us taking a different path. I had a light and followed the path. I saw three deer that day. It was a long arduous journey on foot. I got rocks and thorns in my boots and, to top things off, it was pouring rain and 40 degrees outside. But I stayed on the path.

On the other hand, my friend departed from the path. I would later learn that he experienced even greater challenges. Apparently, he'd heard coyotes nearby, became scared, and began to run in the dark. A few times he was cornered by the thick brush which was packed with thorns that cut him up. After pushing through the brush several times in the dark, he looked down and noticed that his pants were gone. Yes, you read that correctly–his pants were gone. My roommate told me that only remnants of his waistband remained! At this point he realized he was not going hunting that day. He turned around and ran to his truck–with no pants. Not only did he not hunt, but his morning was spent running in fear because he left the path.

Psalm 119 talks about our paths being lighted and being obvious—but it says nothing about our path being easy. A common misconception Christians have is that the path God has for us will be easy—but that can't be found anywhere in Scripture. In fact, we find the opposite: a promise that things will be difficult, but that God will be with us. God will be our strength. And there is a repeated theme throughout Scripture that God's Word will light up our paths and the direction we should take will be obvious.

As we have been focusing on God's Word, you have likely already found the decisions you were struggling with on Day 1 have become much clearer.

Think About It:

- Is God asking me to do something that is difficult?

- What things have been made more obvious over these last 15 days?

- When I focus on what I know from the Bible, what action(s) come to mind?

Pray:

Heavenly Father, thank You for lighting my path. Help me to focus on Your Word and to be led by it each step of the way.

Walk It Out:

As you have read over these passages and walked out the steps, I am confident God has made at least one thing obvious to you over these 15 days. Whatever it is, whether it be forgiving someone, sharing Jesus, serving in your community, or even asking a certain someone out on a date—if God has made it obvious, DO IT!

Notes:

_____

_____

_____

_____

_____

_____

DAY 16

TRUST

Trust in the Lord with all your heart
And do not lean on your own understanding.
-Proverbs 3:5, NASB

When I worked in college ministry, it was not a paying gig. I would work 60 hours a week at a sports store to pay the bills and then put in the equivalent of full-time hours leading a college ministry. This was the busiest I've ever been in my life, and I knew it was not a sustainable lifestyle. Two years into this routine, God spoke to me through an individual—specifically, the testimony from a drummer of a praise band. He said that before drumming on a praise band, he wasn't doing anything wrong with his life. He was following Jesus. Then one-day God convicted him he could do more for Jesus. So, he became a drummer for a Christian band and began to drum for Jesus as his job.

Such a simple testimony, but it penetrated my spirit. Here I was, spending 60 hours a week at a sports store when God called me to something else entirely—college ministry.

This is where trust comes in; I had no income outside of the sports store. It took a lot of faith and trust in the Lord to do this—to quit a full-time, good-paying job to focus on ministry that doesn't pay anything. I did not know how God was going to provide.

I trusted God and I went to my boss, planning to quit. Before I could get a word out, she told me, "I have great news! Corporate has seen how sales have increased nearly 40% and they are building you a new store!" I was the head store manager; I received a commission on all store sales. A new, larger store meant a much larger check each week. I said, "Wow," in the most unexcited way you have ever heard. I did not know how to respond. I'd like to tell you I quit my job that day, but I didn't. The path God had for me and the direction where I should focus my energy were obvious. However, I struggled to trust God to provide. I had tremendous difficulty not leaning on my own understanding.

Eventually I did quit, and I did do what God was asking of me. Guess what? God provided! I got another job, working only six hours a week, but paying 4x the hourly wage of the sports store. Trust in the Lord with all your heart!

Think About It:

- Am I willing to trust God with my whole heart?

- How do I not lean on my understanding, and trust God's leading instead?

- Are there things I'm holding onto—things God is telling me to let go of to lean more on Him?

Pray:

Father, search my heart and mind and reveal to me the things I might be holding back and any hindrances that may keep me from trusting You with my whole heart. (Spend at least two minutes in silence listening for what God may have to say to you).

Walk It Out:

The hope is that God has used this silence and prayer to reveal something for you to give up or surrender. It was four months before I was able to give up the sports job. Letting go can be a process. Start the process of bringing before God what you need to release right now!

Notes:

_____

_____

_____

_____

_____

_____

_____

DAY 17

TEST YOUR FAITH

For my thoughts are not your thoughts,
neither are your ways my ways, declares the Lord.
-Isaiah 55:8, ESV

My first overseas mission trip was an act of obedience. I did not understand why God wanted me to go. This was just after I had quit the sports store to focus on ministry, and I had no income. I was 25 years old. Financially, it made no sense to go on a mission trip at the time. I did not know the language of the people where God was sending me. I was not particularly gifted at sharing Jesus, and I already had a calling to the ministry I was running. But God made it clear—He lit the path and made it straight. Go to a country in Asia where the Gospel is not allowed to be talked about, God said, and talk about it.

It started with meeting one missionary from the country, followed by another missionary from the same country. During that summer, my pastor returned from work in that same country. I also had dreams about going to this country. I began to pray about this place. Through sermons and people, God kept bringing up this one nation. There are so many instances, it is hard to list them all. I remember one elder in my church kept asking if I had a passport yet. Looking back, I realize he was asking for an entirely different reason but, at the time, all I heard was God pointing me to the same country. One day I was talking with my friends about this when one friend yelled, "Why aren't you going?" I said, "I guess it comes down to the money." The next day I received an unexpected and large check from the government! I went to that country and did evangelism with college students.

I went out of obedience, but I did not understand why God wanted me to go. I was quickly amazed at how many people there spoke English. God was able to use me right away. The people there had this hunger for the truth that, honestly, people in the U.S do not have. Of the 12 people I was able to share with in my time there, only one had heard the name of Jesus prior to my arrival. God's reason for bringing me to that country became obvious.

Do not expect to understand everything God asks of you. Take a leap of faith.

Think About It:

- How do I distinguish God's voice from my thoughts?

- Why are God's ways often mysterious to me?

- Do I ever have difficulty trusting God's direction because I don't understand it?

Pray:

Father God, may my thoughts and ways more closely resemble Your thoughts and ways. I want to follow You faithfully even when I lack understanding.

Walk It Out:

As you have submitted your plans before God, and He has given you answers that may be beyond your understanding, continue with these issues in prayer. Share all these things with a more mature Christian— perhaps a leader in your church. Ask God to continue to make your path straight and obvious.

Notes:

_____

_____

_____

_____

_____

_____

_____

_____

DAY 18

SOCKS AND SANDALS

In all your ways acknowledge to him,
and he will make your paths straight.
-Proverbs 3:6, ESV

Back when I was in youth group, I had a friend who usually dressed very fashionably. But one day at church my friend showed up wearing socks with sandals—an obvious fashion no-no. The youth pastor was about to start Bible study when he turned to my friend and, looking at his feet, asked, "What were you thinking?" I thought my friend's answer was profound. He said, "I was getting ready for church…" and continued with a detailed description. I will spare you the entire reply, but basically, he explained his shirt and pants selection and so on. Then as he was about to put on his shoes, he asked himself, "What would Jesus do?" He thought, "I don't believe Jesus had sneakers. It was probably more like sandals, so I should wear sandals." And he finished telling his story to the youth group by saying, "And my socks were already on so I wore socks and sandals because I thought that's what Jesus would do." As silly as that may sound,

I've often worn socks and sandals since then as a reminder to acknowledge God in the little things.

Thinking about God in the little things will help you weed out negative activities. If we cannot acknowledge God in something, it needs to go. This is an area I still struggle with. I talk with God throughout the day. I praise Him for little blessings. But I know I lack here because if I truly acknowledged God in everything, I would be more careful about what things I let into my life through TV or my phone. For example, some of the movies I have seen and some of the music I have listened to are not God-honoring. Even in things I read, I fall short from time to time.

I think there's great significance in acknowledging God when you put on your shoes, or turn on your music, or stream your video content. Do you do that? Do you talk to God about what you're doing? Think of God as a friend sitting next to you. You don't want to ignore Him because He loves you and He's got your back. Proverbs 3:6 says, "In all your ways acknowledge him, and he will make your paths straight." Again, "straight paths" does not mean easy, it means obvious. God's plan for you can be made obvious.

Think About It:

- How many times each day do I acknowledge God?

- What activities do I do in a day or week where I do not acknowledge God?

- How can I remind myself to acknowledge God throughout the day?

Pray:

Father, I confess I do not acknowledge You in everything. Convict me of what activities need to go and help me to focus on You throughout my day.

Walk It Out:

As you thought through the questions and prayed the prayer above, what stood out to you as something to give up, in order to better live out Proverbs 3:6?

Notes:

_____

_____

_____

_____

_____

_____

_____

_____

DAY 19

STILL SMALL VOICE

And after the fire came a gentle whisper.
-1 Kings 19:12b, NIV

Read 1 Kings 19:11-13

The few times I've gone camping, the thing that always stands out is how many stars you can see at night. Every city has a degree of light pollution that keeps us from seeing the vast number of stars on display in the night sky. Likewise, noise pollution, time pollution, distractions, commitments, and elements of life not centered on Jesus Christ, make us hard-of-hearing toward the voice of God. The passage in 1 Kings says there was a great wind, an earthquake, and even a fire, but it was in the gentle whisper and still small voice that God spoke.

I've moved a lot, even since I was a child. I've moved out-of-state and even out of the country. Likewise, I've had friends move away. That's always been the hardest part of moving: friends we're used to seeing every day are now in a different time zone. It was a loss and an adjustment. All of my best friends suddenly lived on the opposite side of the world. When I ate breakfast, they ate dinner; when I went to bed, they were just waking up. Rarely could I just call a friend on an impulse; I had to be very intentional and plan it out. Nearly 10 years later many of my best friends back then are my best friends now, because I made time for people that matter.

Slow down. Turn down all the noise and distractions in your life. Stop and listen; make quality time for you and God.

Think About It:

- Why did God speak to Moses in a burning bush but Elijah in a whisper?

- What noise pollution do I have in my life?

- How do I expect God to speak to me?

Pray:

Heavenly Father, thank You for speaking to Your people! Help me to be quiet and listen.

Walk It Out:

Write out a plan to turn down the noise pollution in your life and spend quality time with God.

Notes:

_____

_____

_____

_____

DAY 20

HIS VOICE

My sheep hear my voice, and I know them, and they follow me.
-John 10:27, ESV

We know God is a Good Shepherd and He takes care of His sheep—us. This passage tells us He knows us! It tells us we should follow Him. It also says we, as His sheep, hear His voice! If you are following Christ, you are hearing His voice! Knowing His voice is learned through relationship. If you have only been following God a short while, understand that it takes time to discern what His voice is like.

I was 7 years old the first time I used a telephone. I remember calling my best friend's house, and I couldn't distinguish between my best friend Tony's voice and his older brother's voice. At 7 I just didn't pay attention to what his voice sounded like. We were little and didn't have in-depth discussions. We played Nintendo, rode bikes, and shot water guns at each other. As we got older and our relationship matured, we talked about girls, school, family, and everything that was important in our lives. As time passed and I would call Tony's house and someone answered with a simple "hello," I could tell immediately if it was Tony. There wasn't one particular day it suddenly became clear whose voice was whose. It was gradual. I knew Tony's voice better the longer we knew each other. I think the same is true for God's voice.

I am asked so often, what does God's voice sound like? First and foremost, it sounds like the Bible. I don't mean God speaks in "thee and thou" like in the King James Bible. I mean the Bible is literally God Almighty's Words! Furthermore, if God is giving you personal direction, what He says sounds like the Bible. He may answer your question with a question; Jesus did this all the time. You may ask for a provision, and He confronts your sin (John 4). You may be running away, not even trying to talk to Him, and that is when He speaks the loudest (Jonah and Elijah). It always starts with His Word. God has also spoken to me through people, but that is always confirmed by His Word. God definitely speaks in a still, small voice, but I wouldn't pigeonhole God's voice to be quiet. Listen for the gentle whisper, but He also speaks in a burning bush (Exodus 3) and through purple sweaters (Day 11). Get to know God intimately and listen carefully to His voice!

Think About It:

- Think about your time with God versus your time with your best friend. How well should I know His voice in comparison?

- What ways have I heard God's voice?

- How certain am I when I hear from God?

Pray:

Heavenly Father, thank You for knowing me. Help me to recognize and be obedient to Your voice.

Walk It Out:

Summarize what God has been saying to you throughout this book.

_____

_____

_____

_____

_____

_____

_____

_____

_____

_____

_____

_____

DAY 21

COME CLOSER

Come close to God, and God will come close to you. Wash your hands, you sinners; purify your hearts, for your loyalty is divided between God and the world.
-James 4:8, NLT

An invitation has been extended. What will your response be?

The Bible says in the fourth chapter of James, "Come close to God, and he will come close to you." This isn't just reading the Bible or attending church. Consider this passage from James like a date. If you're on a date, you took a chance and asked someone out, or you accepted an invitation to go on a date.

If you accept the invitation and hope for any chance of a relationship, there must be two-way communication. The relationship won't last or grow if you just talk and don't listen. The relationship won't grow if you don't put in the time. It is a two-way street. Draw near to God, and He will draw near to you. The context of this passage is important. If you read the entire fourth chapter of James, it talks about submitting to the Lord, resisting the devil, and fleeing from sin. Amid this passage, telling us to flee from the devil and sin, it says, "Come close to God, and God will come close to you." This brings us closer to our Creator, brings our sin into the light, and gives us freedom from our sins through Jesus Christ.

We are all sinners. Whether it be pride, lust, lies, hate, envy, greed, or many others, we all have sinned numerous times. Is there a sin you are a slave to and can't get away from? Maybe you are a compulsive liar, or you have an addiction to pornography, or you cannot keep your anger under wraps. Maybe you just want so many things you can't have. You've tried to "flee" from these things, but they keep popping back up in your life.

Draw near to God and He will draw near to you. Submit yourself to God, resist the devil, and he will flee. I've had many people tell me stories about how they have "prayed" about a sin or struggle and that God wouldn't deliver them. Here is how a lot of those conversations go:

"I spent—I don't know, two or three minutes praying about that issue."

"I spent a few minutes praying about my porn addiction as I fell asleep."

"I'm in constant prayer about it, like 3 or 4 times a day. I don't have much time because of work and responsibilities, but like 10-30 seconds constantly through the day."

Let us go back to a dating relationship. Would you agree to go on a second date with someone who only talked to you for two minutes? Would you hold someone's hand who had only talked to you in 30-second intervals? That doesn't allow anyone much time to respond and have a conversation. How strong would this dating relationship be if you only talked for 3-4 minutes as you fell asleep?

When the Bible says, come close to God and he will come close to you, it is not talking about a 30-second prayer before a meal or even sitting still for an hour on Sunday. I think it is starting an engaging relationship as you would with a boyfriend or girlfriend. Giving them your attention, time, and devotion. As you do that and flee from sin that entangles you, it becomes easy to see that our relationship with God is quantifiable.

God's plan for you is also knowable and assessable.

I don't mean in a general way, I mean in a very specific, personal way. Whether you should date this person? What college you should go to? Should you take that job?

God has a plan for you. You can know it and you can measure it. You cannot get the plan if you do not know The Guy who has the plan and purpose for your life.

Think About It:

- How have you seen God come closer to you in these 21 days?

- What changes do you feel the Lord prompting you to make?

Pray and thank God for what He has done in these 21 days and what He's going to do moving forward.

Walk It Out:

Looking back at Day 1, review your decision struggles. Some may be clear; others undoubtedly are still in question. Continue to come close to God and watch Him come closer and lead you each step of the way.

You may not have all the answers. That's okay. You know how to find them, and you hear His voice!

Notes:

_____

_____

_____

_____

_____

_____

_____

_____

_____

_____

_____

_____

_____

_____

_____

_____

_____

_____

_____

_____

_____

_____

_____

_____

_____

_____

_____

_____

_____

_____

_____

_____

_____

_____

_____

_____

_____

_____

_____

_____

_____

_____

_____

_____

_____

_____

_____

_____

_____

_____

_____

_____

_____

_____

_____

_____

_____

_____

_____

_____

_____

_____

_____

_____

_____

ABOUT THE AUTHOR

Tim grew up knowing the reality of God from a young age but struggled how to understand His will. After more than fifteen years of seeking Jesus, being transformed by  His Word and Holy Spirit, and serving the Church around the world, he has gained confidence in knowing God's plan for his life. Tim wrote this book to share the wisdom he has gained in understanding God's personal plan for every follower of Christ.

ABOUT KHARIS PUBLISHING:

Kharis Publishing, an imprint of Kharis Media LLC, is a leading Christian and inspirational book publisher based in Aurora, Chicago metropolitan area, Illinois. Kharis' dual mission is to give voice to under-represented writers (including women and first-time authors) and equip orphans in developing countries with literacy tools. That is why, for each book sold, the publisher channels some of the proceeds into providing books and computers for orphanages in developing countries, so that these kids may learn to read, dream, and grow. For a limited time, Kharis Publishing is accepting unsolicited queries for nonfiction (Christian, self-help, memoirs, business, health and wellness) from qualified leaders, professionals, pastors, and ministers. Learn more at: About Us - Kharis Publishing - Accepting Manuscript

CPSIA information can be obtained
at www.ICGtesting.com
Printed in the USA
LVHW051116100322
712843LV00005B/6